SIMPLE **SOLUTIONS**®

House-Training

PLUS **TRAINING TIPS**

BY KIM CAMPBELL THORNTON

BOWTIE PRESS®

A Division of BowTie, Inc.
Irvine, CA

P9-DTE-207

June Kikuchi, Editorial Director

Camille Garcia, Assistant Editor

Roger Sipe, Special Projects Editor

Elizabeth Spurbeck, Assistant Editor

Karen Julian, Publishing Coordinator

Brian Bengelsdorf, Art Director

Copyright © 2002, 2009 by BowTie Press®. Cover image of black Labrador Retriever by Gina Cioli & Pamela Hunnicutt/BowTie Inc. Interior photos by Isabelle Francais/BowTie Inc.

All rights reserved. No part of this book may be reproduced, stored in a retrieval system, or transmitted in any form or by any means, electronic, mechanical, photocopying, recording, or otherwise, without the prior written permission of BowTie Press®, except for the inclusion of brief quotations in an acknowledged review.

The Library of Congress has cataloged the earlier edition as follows:
Thornton, Kim Campbell.
  House-Training / by Kim Campbell Thornton ; illustrations by Buck Jones.
      p. cm. — (Simple solutions)
ISBN-10: 1-889540-84-6 (paperback : alk. paper)
ISBN-13: 978-1-889540-84-9 (paperback : alk. paper)
1. Puppies—Training I. Title. II. SimpleSolutions.
  SF431 .T53 2002
  636.7'0887—dc21

                              2002005296

BowTie Press®
A Division of BowTie, Inc.   Printed and bound in China.
3 Burroughs, Irvine, California 92618   15 14 13 12 11 10 09   1 2 3 4 5 6 7 8 9 10

Contents

Secrets to Success

SIMPLE SOLUTIONS

uppies pee. And poop. A lot. And often. If you've never lived with a puppy, you'll be amazed by the number of times your little fur ball will need to go potty. Every hour or two, he will start sniffing and circling, looking for a place to do his business. If you aren't watchful, accidents can happen frequently.

Not surprisingly, house-training is the first lesson new owners must teach their pups, and rightfully so: House-training is the foundation for good behavior. Without it, dogs can't become members of the family, and they run the risk of being exiled to the backyard, never getting the attention and social interaction that they need, deserve and crave.

Happily, the secrets to successful house-training are simple: Time, patience, consistency and supervision are all that are needed.

Puppies are quick learners. A regular potty schedule, combined with praise for going in the right spot, will help them get the right idea. Dogs are naturally clean animals, and they don't want to soil their living area. House-training teaches dogs that the house is the living area and the yard (or whichever spot you choose) is the potty area.

Just as with children, potty-training a puppy is a process. It's not something a puppy can learn in a day or even a week. It might take a few weeks just for your dog to understand what you want. However, until your puppy

Breeds with Potty Problems

A number of breeds are more difficult to house-train than others, including many small breeds, such as Chihuahuas, Yorkies, Papillons, Italian Greyhounds, Shih Tzu and Toy Poodles. Other breeds that are known to be tough to potty-train are Bichon Frise, Maltese, Havanese and Bolognese, as well as some hounds (Beagles, Afghan Hounds, Salukis, Harriers and foxhounds) and small terriers (Jack Russell Terriers and Soft Coated Wheaten Terriers). These dogs need extra supervision and a lot of positive reinforcement.

Your pup can't hold his bladder for more than four hours. Creating a potty schedule will work to your —and his—advantage.

is 4 to 6 months old, he's not physiologically capable of "holding it" for more than about four to six hours. A puppy's muscle control isn't fully developed yet, and his bladder is not large enough to hold it any longer than that.

Remember that each dog is an individual. Some pups are potty-trained at 3 months, while others may not be completely reliable until they're 9 months to 1 year old.

If you acquire your puppy at 8 weeks of age, expect to take him outside at least six to eight times a day. By the time he's about 6 months old, potty trips will be down to three or four times a day.

A rule of thumb is to take your puppy out in hourly intervals equal to his age in months. For instance, a 2-month-old puppy should go out every two hours, a 4-month-old every four hours, and a 6-month-old every six hours. This can vary, of course, depending on the individual dog: Some young puppies need to go out every half-hour. It's your responsibility to make sure your pup gets plenty of opportunities to go potty in the correct spot.

Other good rules to follow include taking your pup out first thing in the morning — yes, even before you have your first cup of coffee — and 10 to 30 minutes after every meal, when he wakes from a nap, after every play session, and just before he goes to bed for the night.

That's a lot of dog walks! How can you fit them all in? What if everyone in your family works or goes to school?

Those things are important, but so is your puppy's potty schedule, especially during the first couple of weeks he's with you. **Without a schedule, your puppy can't learn what he needs to know**. Try to go home once or twice during the day, hire a dog walker or a pet sitter, or ask a friend or neighbor to take your dog out for a walk so he can potty. Try taking time off work during the first week of house-training to firmly establish the schedule and rules in your pup's mind. It's helpful to start training on a weekend or during a long holiday.

Time to Get Started

SIMPLE SOLUTIONS

Start house-training your puppy as soon as you bring him home. Even before you invite him into the house, take him to the potty spot you've chosen and let him sniff around. Make note of any patterns of sniffing, circling and/or squatting. These are clues that he needs to go out. If he performs, praise him in a happy tone of voice, saying "Good potty!" Then, take him inside and introduce him to his special place, such as a crate or playpen.

Young puppies should not have the run of the house. Before you bring your puppy home, choose a safe area of the house to let your pup stay. This is usually a kitchen, laundry room, bathroom or some other area with an

SIMPLE SOLUTIONS

Paper-Training

Most trainers agree that teaching a puppy to potty on paper and then retraining her to potty outside can be confusing. Some dogs never quite figure out that they're supposed to move on from papers to the great outdoors, and they mistakenly continue to potty on any pile of papers they see. However, if you live in a high-rise or you're unable to walk your dog regularly, paper-training may be your only choice.

To paper-train your dog, spread a few layers of paper in the area you want your pup to go. Then, instead of taking her outside, take her to the papers and let her sniff around. If she moves off the papers, set her back on them. When she eliminates, praise her.

If you're having trouble getting your pup to use the papers, try holding a sponge underneath your dog to capture some of her urine. Then, use the sponge to scent the papers. The next time you take your pup to the papers, she'll smell her urine and remember what she's supposed to do. You also can purchase pads at pet-supply stores that claim to induce eliminating. When the pee pad is placed on the papers, its scent is supposed to encourage the puppy to eliminate there.

Constant supervision on your **part** is another important element in successful house-training.

uncarpeted floor. Rooms with tile, vinyl or concrete floors are good choices.

Lay down papers in this room (this is not paper-training but simply an easier way to clean up messes). Put your pup's open crate, a couple of chew toys and a food and water dish at the opposite end of the room. Close off the room with a baby gate or other barrier to prevent him from wandering throughout the house. **Until your puppy is house-trained, he needs to be under your direct supervision or confined to an area where he can't get into trouble**.

The goal is for your pup to eliminate away from his crate and eating area whenever you aren't there to take him out. Once your pup is consistently eliminating in a certain spot on the papers, you can gradually take up the papers, leaving only the favored area covered.

If you come home and your pup has pottied in the safe room, don't scold him. He's just doing what comes naturally. Take him outside and praise him when he potties in the chosen spot. **If you take him to the same area every time, the lingering scent will prompt him to go again**.

After your puppy eliminates, say "Good potty!" or something else that comes across as praise. Choose any short phrase that works for you, and say it in a happy, approving tone of voice. When you assign a name to the action, your puppy learns to associate the word or phrase with the act and may learn to go on cue. Just don't make

Litter-Training

You can also train your dog to use a litter box. Take your puppy to the litter box first thing in the morning, after every meal, after naptime and playtime, and just before bedtime. If she jumps out of the litter box, put her back in until she goes. When she pees or poops, praise her.

Litter boxes and litter suited for puppies and dogs who weigh up to 35 pounds can be found in pet-supply stores. Shredded paper, which some dogs prefer, also can be substituted for litter.

Pay attention to your dog's behavior before he potties, such as sniffing or circling, so you'll know when he has to go.

the mistake one owner did of using the phrase "Good dog" or your pup will start going potty every time you praise him, whether you meant him to or not! **Make sure everyone in the family knows the key phrase for going potty and uses it consistently**. You don't want your puppy to become confused.

Speed up the training process by **making potty time pleasant for your puppy**. Keep some tiny treats in your pocket so you can reward him the instant he's through eliminating. (Don't interrupt him before he's finished, though.) Then, spend a few minutes playing. He'll soon learn that the quicker he does his business, the sooner playtime comes. This is useful on rainy days or when you're in a hurry.

The
Great
Crate
Debate

SIMPLE SOLUTIONS

Dogs are den animals, which means they like small, cozy spots — much like the caves of their wild ancestors — where they can curl up and feel safe. Because most of us can't provide caves for our dogs, a wire or plastic carrier or crate is the next best thing.

Many people don't like the idea of putting their puppy in something that resembles a cage. It seems cruel to them, but just the opposite is true. **Placing your puppy in a crate when you can't be there to watch him keeps him safe and out of trouble**. When he's in his crate, he can't nibble on the wallpaper, pee on your favorite rug or get into the trash. That means you won't come home

A crate should serve as a safe haven for your dog, so be sure to encourage positive associations.

Crate No-Nos

Keep in mind that crates can be misused. Your pup should never be confined to his crate for more than three or four hours at a time during the day. It is cruel to leave a young pup in a crate all day long when no one is at home. It's counterproductive and leaves your puppy no choice but to eliminate in the crate, which defeats the crate's purpose in house-training. The crate is meant to be your pup's den, and if she learns to soil the crate, it will be even more difficult to house-train her. (Be aware that crate-training often does not work with puppies from pet stores because they have learned that eliminating in a cage is normal.) If you have to leave your pup for an extended period of time, put the open crate in a safe room as described above.

It's important that the crate not be used as a place of punishment. Never crate your puppy in anger. Her crate should always be a safe haven where she can go for a nap or to get away from the tugging fingers of toddlers. Be sure your children know that the crate is the dog's special room where she's not to be bothered.

and get mad at him for doing what puppies do: explore, destroy, chew and eliminate. Some people place a dog crate or puppy playpen in several different rooms, such as the living room, bedroom and home office, so the puppy always has a safe place to go to. Just be sure to keep one in the area where the family spends most of its time because your puppy will want to be close by.

Your job is to reduce your puppy's chances of making a mistake, and a crate is a good way to accomplish that. Using a crate is much kinder than banishing a dog to the basement, garage or backyard so that he never learns how to be responsible in the house. Plus, the cost of a crate is much less than the cost of repairing chewed-up furniture.

A crate should be just large enough for your dog to stand up, turn around and stretch out on his side. If the crate is too big, your pup will be able to eliminate at one end of the crate and sleep at the other. If your puppy is going to grow into a large adult, buy a crate suited to his adult size but block off part of it with a box or divider. As your pup grows, increase the amount of space he has in the crate until a divider is no longer needed.

To teach your puppy that the crate is a happy place, give him a treat each time he goes inside. As he steps inside, say "Crate!" or "Bed!" in a happy tone of voice. It's always a good idea to assign a name to each action you want your puppy to learn. Soon, he'll go racing to his crate whenever you say the magic word. Be sure to reward him with praise and a treat, and leave a safe chew toy inside for him to play with. **Place the crate in a busy area of the house such as the den or kitchen so he doesn't feel abandoned when he's in it**. You can feed your puppy in the crate, which is also a good way to increase your pup's positive association with the crate.

At night, let your pup sleep in his crate next to your bed. He'll be comforted by your presence, and in the morning, you'll be aware of any restlessness indicating he's ready to go out. It's important to avoid teaching your puppy that whining or barking will get him released from the crate. Wait until he's quiet before opening the door.

Your puppy should be able to go the entire night without an accident, especially if he's more than 3 months old. (If your pup does need to go out in the middle of the night, put him right back in his crate after he has pottied so he learns that nighttime isn't playtime.)

Plastic crates make traveling a breeze. Plus, they'll make your pup less nervous during his first few car trips.

Stay on Schedule

SIMPLE SOLUTIONS

Watching your puppy when he's outside his safe place is crucial. If you don't watch him, you won't be able to prevent accidents. A good way to keep your puppy from wandering off and having an accident while your back is turned is to leash him and keep him at your side. He'll enjoy being with you, and you'll notice immediately if he needs to go out. Give him a toy to play with while he's next to you. If you're doing something that doesn't allow you to keep a close watch on your puppy, put him in his crate, playpen or safe room. This will help prevent any potty accidents.

Every time you notice your puppy sniffing, circling or squatting, clap your hands to get his attention and say something like "Outside? Do you need to go outside?" Then, hustle him out before he has a chance to do anything. Set a timer so that you remember to take him out every hour or two, even if he doesn't show any signs of needing to go out.

Always take your pup out on a leash so you can see him potty, and praise him when he does. Giving a food reward, such as a bit of kibble, immediately after your pup potties further reinforces the habit of eliminating outdoors. Consistent positive reinforcement is the key to successful house-training.

It's very important that you go outside with your puppy. If you aren't there with him, you can't praise him for eliminating or teach him the "go potty" cue. You also have no way of knowing whether he actually did anything.

Many dog owners get angry because they send their puppy outside only to have the dog pee or poop when he comes back inside the house. Without your guidance, your pup won't understand why he's outside. If he hasn't performed after 15 or 20 minutes, take him inside and crate him. Try again later.

Another way to help your puppy potty on schedule is to feed him at set times throughout the day rather than leaving food out and allowing him to nibble all day

Surface Smarts

Dogs develop preferences for certain potty surfaces, usually based on what they learn as a puppy. It's a good idea to expose your pup to different potty surfaces such as asphalt, concrete and gravel so that if you don't have access to grass, you won't have a problem getting her to go.

A sound diet of high-quality food will help your dog's digestive system and need to eliminate.

long. When your dog eats at the same time every day, it's easier to gauge when he'll need to go out. Feed your young pup after his first elimination of the day, once in mid afternoon and again in the evening, spacing his meals about six hours apart. Feeding your pup high-quality, highly digestible food will help keep him on schedule as well. The ingredients in these foods produce less stool volume, meaning your puppy won't have to eliminate as often.

Eating stimulates your pup's bowels, so take him outside after every meal. Give him a couple of minutes to do his business, and if he doesn't potty, take him back inside and crate him so that he doesn't potty in the house. Try again in 10 minutes. Keep taking him out at 10-minute intervals until he eliminates. **Pay attention to how much time elapses between the end of the meal and when he finally potties**. Most pups need to go 30 to 60 minutes after eating. If you know your pup's needs, you can keep him on schedule and avoid accidents.

To establish a potty routine, take your puppy outside after every meal, water break and play session.

Accidents Happen

SIMPLE SOLUTIONS

our puppy is bound to make mistakes, especially in the first few weeks of house-training. Always remember that he is just a baby — no matter what his size — and that he needs time to learn. You are his teacher, and he relies on you to make sure that he gets plenty of opportunities to do things right.

If your pup pees or poops in the house, don't yell at him. Instead, make a note to yourself to watch him more closely and take him out more frequently. Then, gently put him in his crate or the safe room, and clean up the mess. **Remember: Reward correct behavior and ignore unwanted behavior.** Never rub his nose in the mess or swat him with a rolled-up newspaper. Not only will anger and negative punishment increase stress and fear in your puppy, he'll also become sneaky about finding places to potty.

If you catch your puppy in the act of eliminating in the house, clap your hands to get his attention and say something like "*Aaaaght*! Outside." If he stops (which is unlikely), take him outside to finish. Avoid saying "no" or calling him a bad dog. You don't want him to think that the act of eliminating is wrong, you just want your puppy to know that he chose the wrong place.

Until your pup is reliable, don't let him run free in your home. A puppy who eliminates everywhere in the house has too much freedom. Instead, keep him by your

Don't scold your puppy when he makes a mistake. He won't make the connection. Instead, keep a closer eye on him so you can read his potty signs.

Potty Bell

Part of house-training is being able to read your pup's cues. Dogs have different ways of letting you know when they need to go out. Some dogs bark or run to the door; others are subtle in their communication, which they limit to staring or twitching their ears a certain way.

Some dogs can learn to ring a bell when they want to go out. To teach this trick, hang a bell on the doorknob or on the wall next to the door. Be sure it's within your pup's reach. Every time you take her out for a potty run, ring the bell before you go out the door. When she rings the bell on her own, praise her and take her out. She will eventually learn to ring the bell on her own.

side or confined to his safe room or crate. This is especially important during the busiest times of the day such as mornings and dinner time, when you have less time to keep a close eye on him. It is important to restrict your puppy's access to certain areas within the house until he starts eliminating outdoors on a regular basis.

If you're having some problems house-training your puppy, **make sure you're being consistent with your training methods**. Don't try method after method, quickly switching from one to another. Choose the method you want to use and stick with it. Otherwise, your puppy will become confused, and a confused canine will not become a happily house-trained hound!

Keep in mind, too, that house-training accidents —
especially after your puppy seems reliable — may indicate
a health problem. Take your puppy to your veterinarian for
an exam if he suddenly breaks house-training for no ap-
parent reason. He may have a bladder or kidney infection.

Don't let your puppy get distracted when he's supposed to be pottying. Keep play time separate.

Cleaning Up

SIMPLE SOLUTIONS

here's a technique to removing stains and odors caused by puppy waste. If done properly, your carpet can look and smell as good as new.

When you're dealing with urine, the first step is to sop up as much of the liquid as possible. Keep a supply of ratty old towels on hand for this job. When you've absorbed as much moisture as possible, saturate the spot with the cleanser of your choice. Many pet owners find success using enzymatic-based cleaning products. Others simply use white vinegar.

Accidents will happen, so just clean them up and move on. He didn't mean to piddle on the floor!

A responsible breeder
will already have begun
house-training his puppies,
giving you a leg up on
a successful outcome.

Avoid using ammonia or any cleansers that contain ammonia; ammonia is a component of urine, and its scent will draw your puppy back to that spot again and again.

Once you've applied the cleanser, use a clean towel or rag to blot the soiled area again. Then, get a dry towel, place it over the area and pile some heavy books on top of the towel. The weight of the books will press the towel into the carpet, allowing it to draw out more moisture. Leave the books on the spot overnight or until the area is completely dry. Sprinkle the spot with baking powder to help soak up moisture and vacuum it up when the spot is dry. You can absorb moisture with a wet vacuum, too.

For solid waste, use a towel or rag to pick up as much of the mess as possible. Dump the stool in the toilet, and toss the towel in a bucket for a hot-water wash later. Just as parents keep diaper pails, many pet owners keep a bucket handy to hold the towels and rags used to clean up doggy urine, stool and vomit.

When you've removed as much waste as you can, apply your chosen cleanser and use another towel to soak up any remaining bits of waste. Then, get a clean towel and use a wet vacuum or the book technique described above until the spot is dry. Until your pup is fully house-trained, it's a good idea to have your carpet professionally cleaned regularly.

No More Mess

Use these clean-up tips to get your house clean while aiding your pup in his need to be house-trained.

• If you don't have any professional cleaners on hand, use ¼ cup white vinegar to 1 quart of water.

• Salt will absorb fresh urine and remove some of the scent.

• In a pinch, rubbing the area with a dryer sheet can remove some of the odor.

• White toothpaste can get some tough stains out of carpets.

Most important, be patient. Taking the time to train your puppy properly early on in his life will pay off many times in the years to come.

SIMPLE SOLUTIONS